Budgeting

Charles Klasky

A PACEMAKER® BOOK

Fearon Education
a division of
David S. Lake Publishers
Belmont, California

Senior development editor: Christopher Ransom Miller
Managing editor: Maura Okamoto
Text and cover designer: Terry McGrath
Illustrator: Duane Bibby
Production editor: Robert E. Wanetick
Design manager: Eleanor Mennick

ISBN–0–8224–1111–3

Printed in the United States of America.

1.9 8 7 6

Contents

1 Who Needs to Plan?

Rich Harris and Les Peterson are good friends. They grew up together and went to the same school. Now they work at the same company, making car parts. They even make just about the same pay. But somehow, at the end of each month, Rich always seems to have more money.

Just last week Rich bought a new motorcycle. Poor Les. He had dreamed of having one like it, but he didn't think it was possible. Later that week, on Thursday, Rich suggested they go out to lunch, but Les said no. He said he had too much work. The truth was he had too little money.

WORDS TO LEARN

budget a plan to help you control how you spend your money; to make a spending plan.

financial problems problems that you have with managing your money, such as not being able to buy something that you need or not being able to pay your bills on time.

There is a simple reason why Rich seems to have more money. Rich uses a **budget**. Each month, Rich plans carefully how he will spend his money. Then he sticks to his plan.

Les, on the other hand, never keeps a budget. Like many people, Les is afraid of living on a budget. He is afraid it will mean he'll have to "pinch pennies" or worry about every cent he spends. And he thinks a budget will be too much work.

"I used to feel the same way," Rich told Les. "But that was before I knew what a budget is or how a budget works. A budget is just a spending plan. It's a way to keep control of your money. And a budget helps you get the things you need and buy the things you want."

Looking at Rich's new motorcycle, Les could see that budgeting had helped his friend. Les knew he earned the same amount of money as Rich. But the only motorcycle Les rode was in his dreams. He decided it was time to find out more about budgeting.

Rich told Les that the first thing you have to do is decide that you really want to keep a budget. Sticking to a spending plan can be hard at first. Sometimes you have to say no to things that you really want to do. But it's people who make budgets work. The very best spending plan won't work if you don't promise yourself you'll stick to it.

After you have decided to keep a budget, the next step is to figure out what your **financial problems** are. Making a list of these money problems isn't as easy as it sounds. You have to ask yourself tough questions. And you have to give yourself true answers.

"Are there some things that I spend too much money on each month?"

"Are there things I need but can't buy because I don't have enough money?"

"Are there bills I can't pay on time?"

"Are there things I buy that I don't really need?"

"Do I have extra money in case something goes wrong?"

You can think of other questions yourself. Your answers to questions like the ones on page 3 will help you make a list of your financial problems. Here is the list that Les made.

1. I don't always have enough money for my rent when it is due.

2. Sometimes I run short of money at the grocery store.

3. I don't have any money in the bank.

4. When I want to buy a present for a friend, I don't always have enough money to get something nice.

5. My car needs new tires, but I can't pay for them right now.

6. I still owe my doctor some money.

7. I would like to buy a green sports jacket to match my orange pants.

FIGURE IT OUT

Do you always have enough money when you need it? Or do you sometimes have financial problems?

Make a list like the one that Les made. Write down several problems you have with managing your money. Some sentences might begin with "I would like to buy . . ." or "Sometimes I don't have enough money to . . ." or "I spend too much money on. . . ."

_____

_____

_____

_____

_____

_____

_____

_____

_____

_____

_____

_____

_____

_____

_____

_____

Les didn't have enough money to do something or to buy something he wanted. These are the kinds of money problems that most people have. Like most people, you can solve many problems like these by keeping a budget.

But don't expect too much from a budget. Keeping a budget won't make you rich. And it won't solve all your money troubles right away. But making a spending plan and sticking to it can help you get control over your money.

Deciding to keep a budget and figuring out where you have trouble managing your money are just the first steps. In Chapter 2, you will see the next step when Les figures out the things he really wants to spend money on.

2 What Do You Want?

When Rich and Les started talking about budgets, Rich asked Les what he planned to do with the money he was earning.

Les didn't understand what Rich meant. "I just buy what I can pay for when I can pay for it," Les told Rich.

Somehow, Les's answer did not surprise Rich. "Many people don't have plans for what they are going to do with their money," Rich said. "But knowing what you are going to do with your money is important. It's one of the first things you must do if you ever want to get control over your money."

WORDS TO LEARN

financial goal something you plan for or want to do with your money, such as buying a car.

goal something you plan for and work toward; something you want. Your goals are based on your values.

value something you think is important, such as keeping your word or getting a good education.

When Rich asked Les what he wanted to do with his money, Rich was really asking Les what his **goals** were. Goals are the things that people want. You may want to have a certain kind of job five years from now, so that you can make a lot more money. You may want to travel to faraway places someday because it would be exciting. These are goals. It's good to have goals. They help to give your life a direction. And people are more likely to get what they want if they know where they are going.

The goals Rich was talking about were **financial goals**. Financial goals are like any other goals. They are what a person plans for and works toward, things that a person wants very much. They are called financial goals because you need money to make them happen.

How do you know what you really want? The first step is to ask yourself what is important to you. The things that are important to you are your **values**. And your values are really what determine your goals. If having a college education is important to you, then one of your goals might be to save up enough money to go to college. If making a lot of money is what you want, then one of your goals might be to train for a job that is high paying. If you want to have children, then one of your goals might be to buy a house for your family to live in.

Les wasn't really sure what his values or goals were. With Rich's help, though, Les was able to figure out some of his values and goals. Rich told Les to begin by making lists of all the things he wanted to have and all the things he wanted to do. This sounded like a good idea to Les. It seemed much easier to him than thinking up what his goals were. Les wrote *What I Want to Have* at the top of one piece of paper. At the top of another piece of paper, Les wrote *What I Want to Do*. It turned out that Les thought of many things he wanted to have besides the "Time Trap" game. He also thought of many things he wanted to do. Below are the two lists that Les made.

What I Want to Have

"Space Race" game

"Sky Divers" game

"Time Trap" game

Enough money to pay my rent on time each month

A color television for my electronic games

Enough money to buy groceries all month long and not run short of money

A new motorcycle like Rich's

A college education

Money in the bank

New tires for my car

A green sports jacket to match my green pants

What I Want to Do

Take a trip to Europe

Take music lessons

Become a famous rock-and-roll star

Take night classes at college

Go out to lunch once a week with Rich

Go skiing every other weekend during the winter

Be able to buy a present when I need to

Pay my doctor the money I owe him

What Les had written were his financial goals. Everything on his lists were things that he wanted to do or have. And everything on his lists depended on money. Les wanted to have enough money so that his life ran smoothly. He had to be able to pay his rent on time. And he wanted to have enough money whenever he had to buy groceries. By looking at his lists, Les could see that there were things that he wanted to be able to buy, such as a motorcycle. Also, his list showed him that there were some things he wanted to be able to do in the future.

FIGURE IT OUT

Make a list of things that you want to have and a list of things that you want to do. If you have trouble getting started with your lists, look back at the things Les listed on page 9.

What I Want to Have

_____

_____

_____

_____

_____

_____

_____

_____

_____

_____

_____

What I Want to Do

_____

_____

_____

_____

_____

_____

_____

_____

_____

_____

_____

WORDS TO LEARN

long-term goals what you want to be able to buy or to do in a long time, such as several months or more than a year.

short-term goals what you want to be able to buy or to do in a short time, either right away or within a few months.

When you set financial goals, it is important to think carefully about those goals. You may dream of owning your own boat or a fancy vacation home. But you need to ask yourself if such things are possible for you to buy with the amount of money you earn. Setting reasonable goals will keep you from falling short of any one goal.

Another thing to think of is how long it will take you to reach each goal. Some things on Les's list of goals, such as being able to pay the rent on time, were things that Les really needed. Other things, such as a color television for his electronic games, were things that Les wanted but didn't really need—at least not right away. Goals that you need to take care of right away or in the near future are called **short-term goals**. Paying the rent on time and paying your monthly bills are both examples of short-term goals.

Goals that can wait for a longer time are called **long-term goals**. So are large goals that you don't really need but that you would like to have or to do. Visiting friends who live far away, getting a new car, and buying a house are examples of long-term goals. Long-term goals are important to have, but some of these goals may have to wait until you meet more pressing short-term goals.

Les separated the goals he listed into the two lists below.

Short-Term Goals	Long-Term Goals
Buying a new game like "Space Race" or "Time Trap"	Buying a color television
Paying the rent each month	Doing skiing every other weekend during the winter
Buying groceries when I need to	Taking a trip to Europe
Going to lunch once a week with Rick	Taking music lessons
Paying the telephone bill, the gas bill, and the electric bill	Getting a new motorcycle like Rich's
Buying a birthday present for my brother	Going to college to take night classes
Buying a green sports jacket to match my orange pants	

FIGURE IT OUT

Look back at the goals you listed on page 10. Which ones are things you need to have or to do soon? Which ones are things that you can wait a longer time for? List each goal as either a short-term goal or a long-term goal below.

Short-Term Goals

_____

_____

_____

_____

_____

Long-Term Goals

_____

_____

_____

_____

_____

Short-term goals are usually goals that you plan to meet each month. Your long-term goals may take you more than a year to reach. Because of this, it's a good idea to list your long-term goals by the number of years in which you plan to meet them. Below, some of Les's long-term goals are listed according to how long Rich thought it would take Les to meet each one.

One-Year Goals

Buying new tires for the car

Taking music lessons

Going skiing every other weekend during the winter

Two-Year Goals

Going to college to take night classes

Buying a new motorcycle

Buying a color television

Five-Year Goals

Taking a trip to Europe

Dividing your long-term goals like this can help you plan for each one. Now when Les makes out his budget, he can look at his list of goals. For his long-term goals he can see how much time he has to save up the money to do them. Then he can figure out how much money he will need to put aside each month in order to meet those goals.

FIGURE IT OUT

Look back at the long-term goals you listed on page 13. Which ones are goals you can meet in one year? Which ones might take you two years or five years? List them below according to how long you think it might take you to reach each one. Don't worry about guessing. Even Les needed Rich's help to break his list into one-year, two-year, and five-year goals. For right now, just make the best guess you can. Later, in Chapter 7, you'll take another look at this list.

One-Year Goals

_____

_____

_____

_____

Two-Year Goals

_____

_____

_____

_____

Five-Year Goals

_____

_____

_____

_____

It was important for Les to set some goals. It made him take a serious look at his life. Many of Les's money problems happened because he just bought things whenever he happened to have money. Les's list of goals gave him a better idea of the things he would need money for.

It's important not to take goals too seriously. Many of your goals, both long-term and short-term, will probably change with time. And you might not meet every single goal you set, either. But that doesn't mean you failed. As for Les, he may not make it to Europe in five years. But if he gets control over his money, he may be able to buy that new motorcycle he wants.

It all takes planning. Like all goals, financial goals call for a lot of hard work. But if you plan how to spend your money and stick to your plan, you will reach most of your financial goals.

In the next chapter, you will learn how to start setting up your own spending plan. You'll learn that after setting goals, the next step in budgeting is to see just how much money you really earn.

3
How Much Do You Have?

THAT BANK MAKES ME MAD!

WHY?

BANK

THEY SAID I DON'T HAVE ANY MONEY IN MY CHECKING ACCOUNT.

BUT HOW CAN I BE OUT OF MONEY WHEN I HAVE ALL THESE CHECKS?

It looks as if Les is having a little trouble keeping track of his money. Like many people, Les does not know how much money he has. Maybe this is another reason why Les can't imagine keeping a budget. After all, if you don't know how much money you have, there's no way you can know how much money you can spend.

Each time he gets a paycheck, Les puts some of that money into the bank. But sometimes he forgets how much he has in the bank. And he never keeps track of how much money he carries around with him. Often, he carries much more than he needs, just to be sure he has enough. And sometimes he runs out of money before he gets his next paycheck.

WORDS TO LEARN

annual salary the amount of money you earn from a job each year.

hourly wage a steady amount of money you are paid for each hour you work.

income money that is given to you, usually as pay for doing some kind of work.

monthly salary the amount of money you earn from a job each month.

pay period a period of time, such as two weeks, in which you work and for which you are paid in your paycheck.

steady income a regular amount of income that does not change each pay period.

In order to know how much money you have, you need to have a good idea of what your **income** will be each month. There are two kinds of income, or ways people earn money. One kind is called a **steady income**. It is called "steady" because it is a regular amount of money that a person earns each **pay period**, which may be a week, two weeks, or a month. For instance, Rich's sister Meg earns $6.00 an hour. This is Meg's **hourly wage,** or the amount of money she earns each hour. Because Meg works the same number of hours each pay period, she has a steady income. She is paid the same amount in each paycheck.

People who earn a steady income know exactly how much they will be paid each pay period. In Meg's case, since she works an 8-hour day, she makes $48.00 each day.

$6.00 an hour $\times$ 8 hours = $48.00 a day

Meg gets a paycheck every 2 weeks. Since she works 5 days a week, there are 10 working days in Meg's pay period. That means that she earns $480.00 each pay period.

$48.00 a day $\times$ 10 days = $480.00 a pay period

Since there are 2 pay periods in almost every month, Meg earns a steady income of $960.00 a month. This is her **monthly salary**.

$480.00 a pay period $\times$ 2 pay periods a month = $960.00 a month

Since Meg is paid every 2 weeks, and there are 52 weeks in a year, she has 26 pay periods a year. Her **annual salary**, or how much she earns each year, is $12,480.00.

$480.00 a pay period $\times$ 26 pay periods = $12,480.00 annual salary

People earning a steady income won't earn any less than they are supposed to unless they take some time off without pay. They won't earn any more than they are supposed to unless they work extra hours in that pay period.

If a person works at a job with a steady income, it is easy to figure out how much money that person will be earning. No matter what kind of steady income a person earns or what the pay period is, you can always figure out how much a person makes for a given period of time.

For example, suppose Lenny makes a monthly salary of $2,300.00. He has a steady income of $2,300.00 a month. You can figure out Lenny's annual salary, or how much he earns a year, by multiplying his monthly salary by 12. Lenny's annual salary would be $27,600.00.

$2,300.00 a month × 12 months in a year = $27,600.00
annual salary

In the same way, if you know what someone's annual salary is, then you can figure out how much that person earns each month—as long as the annual salary is based on a steady income. All you have to do is divide the annual salary by 12. For instance, if Marta makes an annual salary of $14,400.00, her monthly salary is $1,200.00.

$14,400.00 a year ÷ 12 months in a year = $1,200.00
monthly
salary

FIGURE IT OUT

Answer the questions below about people who earn a steady income.

1. Janet works at a job with a steady income. Her hourly wage is $6.50. Answer the questions below about how much Janet earns.
   a. How much does Janet earn in an 8-hour day?

   _____

   b. How much does Janet earn in a 40-hour week?

   _____

   c. How much does Janet earn in a 4-week month?

   _____

   d. How much does Janet earn in a 52-week year?

   _____

2. Complete the chart below to show how much each person earns each pay period.

Worker	Hourly Wage	Hours Worked in a Pay Period	Steady Income for Each Pay Period
Sara	$6.58	160	_____
William	$5.02	140	_____
Alice	$5.50	70	_____
Maria	$4.32	40	_____
Eric	$7.10	80	_____

3. Shirley makes an annual salary of $24,720. How much does Shirley earn each month?

   _____

4. Frank makes a monthly salary of $1,500. What is Frank's annual salary?

   _____

WORDS TO LEARN

base salary   the steady salary that is part of the pay for some workers who are earning a variable income.

commission   earnings based on a percent of the sales a worker makes during a pay period.

percent   a share of something that stands for a part of 100. For example, 5 percent is 5 out of every 100, and 10 percent is 10 out of every 100.

variable income   a changing amount of income that is usually based on how much work you do and how well you do your job.

A **variable income** is one that can change, or vary, from one pay period to another. For instance, if someone earns a variable income, he or she might earn $800 in some pay periods and $700 or $900 in other pay periods. People earning a variable income often don't know how much money they will get with each paycheck.

Some people prefer a variable income because the amount a person makes is based on how often or how well he or she works. Usually, the more or better a person works, the more that person will get paid.

Rich's friend Louis is one person who prefers a job with a variable income. Louis works hard at selling shoes. Like many salespeople, Louis earns a different amount each pay period. He always earns a **base salary**. The company that he works for promises to pay him that amount each pay period. But Louis also earns something called a **commission**. This means that Louis is paid for a **percent** of the amount of products he sells. The more things that Louis sells in a pay period, the more money he makes for the shoe company, and the more money he gets in his paycheck.

Here's how it works. Louis makes a base salary of $200 a week. That is how much he is sure he will make in each one-week pay period that he works. But Louis also earns 5 percent of the money amount of the shoes that he sells. That is his commission. In other words, every time Louis sells $100 worth of shoes, he earns an extra $5 for himself. The chart below gives you a good idea of what Louis could earn in commission selling shoes.

Amount Sold	5 Percent Commission	Amount Sold	5 Percent Commission	Amount Sold	5 Percent Commission
$25.00	$1.25	$200.00	$10.00	$375.00	$18.75
$50.00	$2.50	$225.00	$11.25	$400.00	$20.00
$75.00	$3.75	$250.00	$12.50	$425.00	$21.25
$100.00	$5.00	$275.00	$13.75	$450.00	$22.50
$125.00	$6.25	$300.00	$15.00	$475.00	$23.75
$150.00	$7.50	$325.00	$16.25	$500.00	$25.00
$175.00	$8.75	$350.00	$17.50	$525.00	$26.25

For each pay period, Louis's income equals his base salary plus whatever commission he earned in that pay period.

$200 base salary + commission = Louis's income

If Louis sells $500.00 worth of shoes in one pay period, the amount of his commission will be 5 percent of $500.00. That would mean that his commission would be $25.00.

$500.00 in sales × 5 percent commission = $25.00 commission

His pay for that period would equal his $200.00 base salary plus $25.00 commission. He would earn $225.00.

As with all variable incomes, Louis's amount of income changes according to how well he does his job. Below are two sales record cards that show how Louis's income changed last year from one month to the next.

March					
Pay Period	**Base Salary**	**Amount Sold**	**Commission**	**Money Earned as Commission**	**Weekly Salary**
3/4–3/10	$200.00	$554.02	5 percent	$ 27.70	$227.70
3/11–3/17	$200.00	$339.84	5 percent	$ 16.99	$216.99
3/18–3/24	$200.00	$731.65	5 percent	$ 36.58	$236.58
3/25–3/31	$200.00	$618.54	5 percent	$ 30.93	$230.93
				Monthly Salary:	$912.20

April					
Pay Period	**Base Salary**	**Amount Sold**	**Commission**	**Money Earned as Commission**	**Weekly Salary**
4/1–4/7	$200.00	$932.81	5 percent	$ 46.64	$246.64
4/8–4/14	$200.00	$1,320.21	5 percent	$ 66.01	$266.01
4/15–4/21	$200.00	$821.91	5 percent	$ 41.10	$241.10
4/22–4/28	$200.00	$761.82	5 percent	$ 38.09	$238.09
				Monthly Salary:	$991.84

Louis's lowest pay period came in March. He had just started his job then. For the pay period ending March 17, he sold only $339.84 worth of shoes. His commission was only $16.99, and his weekly salary was $216.99.

By April, Louis knew a little more about the job of selling shoes. Louis's hard work began to pay off. He earned his highest weekly salary in the middle of April. For the pay period ending April 14, he earned $266.01. Louis earned more than usual because he sold more than usual. During that week, he sold $1,320.21 worth of shoes.

Louis's two sales record cards show how much a variable income can change from one month to the next. In April, he earned $79.64 more than he did the month before.

FIGURE IT OUT

Answer these questions about working for a commission.

1. Sharon is a salesperson who works for a commission. Here's Sharon's sales record card for September. Figure out Sharon's commission for each week. (Multiply her amount sold by 2. Then divide by 100.) Then figure out her weekly salaries and her monthly salary.

September					
Pay Period	**Base Salary**	**Amount Sold**	**Commission**	**Money Earned as Commission**	**Weekly Salary**
9/2–9/8	$240.00	$390.50	2 percent		
9/9–9/15	$240.00	$293.91	2 percent		
9/16–9/22	$240.00	$589.02	2 percent		
9/23–9/29	$240.00	$785.00	2 percent		
				Monthly Salary:	

2. Which week did Sharon make the lowest commission? What was her weekly salary for that week?

_____

3. Which week did Sharon make the highest commission? What was her weekly salary for that week?

_____

4. What was Sharon's monthly salary for September?

_____

WORDS TO LEARN

fee a set price that you are paid for doing a certain job.

piecework wages a set price that you are paid for making a certain thing. People working for piecework wages are paid by the piece.

Other kinds of variable incomes include working for a **fee** and working for **piecework wages**. A fee is a set price that someone gets for doing a certain job. For example, Bob charges a fee of $25.00 for mowing lawns and taking care of gardens. It might take Bob one hour to take care of one lawn and garden. Another lawn and garden might take him two hours. But Bob would charge $25.00 for each job. The $25.00 is Bob's gardening fee. If Bob takes care of 3 lawns and gardens a day, he earns $75.00.

$25.00 a lawn × 3 lawns a day = $75.00 a day

If Bob does this same amount of work for 5 days a week, then he earns $375.00 a week.

$75.00 a day × 5 days a week = $375.00 a week

Jane, on the other hand, earns piecework wages. She ties fishing flies and is paid $.50 for each one she makes. If Jane ties 100 flies per week, then she earns $50.00 a week in piecework wages.

$.50 a tied fly × 100 flies a week = $50.00 a week

If Jane wants to make more money, she knows that she must tie more fishing flies or ask for more than $.50 for each one she makes. If Bob wants to earn more money in his gardening job, he has two choices too. He can charge a higher fee if people will pay it. Or he can find more lawns and gardens to take care of each week.

There are many other kinds of jobs in which people earn variable incomes. Waitresses and waiters are one example. They earn a steady salary plus the tips they get. Because of this, their income is different each pay period.

If you earn a variable income, it is important to keep good records of the money you earn. In that way, you will know just how much, or how little, you may be able to spend each month.

FIGURE IT OUT

Answer the questions below about working for a fee and working for piecework wages.

1. Roy decided to paint houses this summer. It takes him a long time and he works hard, so he charges a fee of $1,500.00 for each house he paints.
   a. How much money will Roy earn by painting 2 houses during the summer?

   _____

   b. If Roy wants to earn $6,000.00, how many houses should he paint?

   _____

2. Sally is a car mechanic. She opened her own garage last month. She does tune-ups only, and her fee for each tune-up is $50.00.
   a. How much will Sally make in a week if she tunes up 8 cars?

   _____

   b. If Sally tunes up 8 cars a week, how much money will she earn in a 4-week month?

   _____

   c. How much will Sally make in a week if she tunes up 11 cars?

   _____

   d. If Sally tunes up 11 cars a week, how much money will she earn in a 4-week month?

   _____

   e. After two months, Sally finds out that she needs to earn more money to pay for her garage and other costs. She needs to earn $2,600.00 each month to keep the garage open. If there are 4 weeks in each month, how many tune-ups must Sally do each week?

   _____

3. Dan works as a shirt presser in a laundry. He earns $.50 for each shirt he presses.
   a. How much money will Dan make each hour if he presses 8 shirts an hour?

   _____

   b. How much money will Dan make each hour if he presses 12 shirts an hour?

   _____

   c. How much money will Dan earn in an 8-hour day if he presses 16 shirts an hour?

   _____

FIGURE IT OUT

Draw a line from each statement in List A to the person in List B who said it.

List A

"I make anywhere from $250.00 to $500.00 each week. It all depends on how much I sell. I do know I will get at least $200.00 a week, guaranteed.

"I make $800.00 a month, every month, by working a 40-hour week, every week."

"I get $50.00 for every chair I make. I can usually make two chairs a day. My boss pays me a salary according to how many chairs I make."

"I charge a certain amount of money for each job I complete."

List B

This person has a steady income.

This person earns a variable income and charges a fee for the work he or she does.

This person earns a variable income but also has a base salary.

This person has a variable income and is paid piecework wages.

FIGURE IT OUT

Number of Hours Worked Each Day	
Hourly Wage	
Pay Each Day	
Weekly Salary	
Monthly Salary	
Annual Salary	

Before you can make a budget, you need to have a good idea of how much you earn each month. Complete this page or the next as well as you can and keep it for your own record. You will need the information here when you get to Chapter 5.

- If you earn a steady income, fill in the form at the left. If you have trouble, look back at pages 19 and 20.

- If you earn a variable income, fill in the forms below or on the next page. Fill in the information for three months.

Month:

Pay Period	Fee or Piecework Wage for Each Job Done	Number of Jobs Done Each Week	Weekly Salary
		Monthly Salary:	

Month:

Pay Period	Fee or Piecework Wage for Each Job Done	Number of Jobs Done Each Week	Weekly Salary
		Monthly Salary:	

Month:

Pay Period	Fee or Piecework Wage for Each Job Done	Number of Jobs Done Each Week	Weekly Salary
		Monthly Salary:	

Month:					
Pay Period	**Base Salary**	**Amount Sold**	**Commission**	**Money Earned as Commission**	**Weekly Salary**
			percent		
			percent		
			percent		
			percent		
				Monthly Salary:	

Month:					
Pay Period	**Base Salary**	**Amount Sold**	**Commission**	**Money Earned as Commission**	**Weekly Salary**
			percent		
			percent		
			percent		
			percent		
				Monthly Salary:	

Month:					
Pay Period	**Base Salary**	**Amount Sold**	**Commission**	**Money Earned as Commission**	**Weekly Salary**
			percent		
			percent		
			percent		
			percent		
				Monthly Salary:	

4 What Will You Spend?

YOU KNOW, LES. YOU SHOULD BE MORE CAREFUL ABOUT THE WAY YOU SPEND MONEY.

WHAT DO YOU MEAN? I BUY EVERYTHING ON SALE!

I KNOW, I KNOW.

As you can see, Les is not too careful about how he spends his money. Today, he bought a moose-head clock. Tomorrow, he may not have enough money to put food on the table. Les spends his money carelessly, and he never keeps records of how he spends it. Keeping records of what you spend is important. You can't really keep a budget unless you have a very good idea of how much you spend and what you have paid for.

Rich is more careful about how he spends his money. Unlike Les, Rich keeps a record of everything he pays for each month. This record helps him plan what he will spend each month.

WORDS TO LEARN

expenses things you have to pay for.

fixed expenses expenses that do not change, or that change very little, from month to month.

record of expenses a list of all the expenses, fixed and variable, that you have for a month. Your record of expenses shows how much you spend in a month.

variable expenses expenses that change in amount from one month to the next.

When Rich first started making a budget, he kept a **record of expenses** to show how much he spent each month. The first half of Rich's record of expenses is shown at the top of page 33. It lists Rich's **fixed expenses**. These are **expenses** that cost the same, or very nearly the same, each month. Most of the time, you know how much fixed expenses will cost you. And most of the time, you also know in what part of the month these expenses must be paid.

By looking at Rich's record of fixed expenses, you can see this information:

1 Federal income tax. The first space on Rich's record of expenses is for federal income tax. Most employers withhold, or take out, a certain amount of your salary to pay for federal income tax. If your employer does not do this, then you would need to save part of your salary each month so that you will have enough money to pay your tax when it is due. You would list that monthly amount in this space. The company Rich works for withholds part of his salary to pay for his federal income tax. That's why he hasn't listed any expense in this space for January or February.

2 State income tax. This space is for state income tax. Since Rich's company also withholds part of his salary to pay for his state income tax, he hasn't listed any expense in this space for either month.

3 Property tax. Property tax is listed in this space. If Rich owned a home, he would pay property tax each year. He would want to save a certain amount each month so that he could pay this tax when it was due. If his property tax were $1,200.00 a year, Rich would list an expense of $100.00 in this space for each month. Then, at the end of 12 months, he would have $1,200.00. Since Rich doesn't own a home, he has no property tax to pay.

4 Rent or mortgage payment. In this space, you list your housing expenses. If you are buying a house, you list your monthly mortgage payment, or house payment, here. If you are renting a house or an apartment, you list your monthly rent here. Rich rents an apartment. He has listed an expense of $275.00 for his rent in January and in February.

5 Health insurance. If you pay for your health insurance, that expense is listed in this space. You would list the amount you spend each month. Rich's company pays for his health insurance, so Rich hasn't listed any expense in this space for either month.

		January	February
	FIXED EXPENSES		
1	Taxes: Federal	—	—
2	State	—	—
3	Property	—	—
4	Rent or mortgage payment	275.00	275.00
5	Insurance: Health	—	—
6	Life	19.00	19.00
7	Property	—	—
8	Car	42.15	42.15
9	Loan Payments: Car	91.04	91.04
10	Other *school*	45.00	45.00
11	Emergency savings fund	25.00	25.00
12	**Total of Fixed Expenses**	497.19	497.19

6 Life insurance. Rich's monthly payment for life insurance is listed here. Each month, Rich pays $19.00 for life insurance.

7 Property insurance. Often, people have property insurance for their homes or the things in their apartments. This space is where you would list your expense each month for property insurance. Since Rich has no property insurance, he hasn't listed any expense in this space for either month.

8 Car insurance. Rich pays $42.15 for car insurance each month. He has listed that amount in this space for January and February.

9 Car loan. A couple of years ago, when he bought a car, Rich had to take out a loan to pay for it. He is paying back the loan in payments of $91.04 each month. This is the space where he has listed that amount each month.

10 Other loan. Here, you list any other loan payments you are making each month. It's a good idea also to make a note about what the payments are for. Rich borrowed money to pay for school. He is paying that loan back by paying $45.00 each month. Rich has listed that expense in this space for January and February.

11 Emergency savings fund. In this space, Rich has listed an expense of $25.00 each month. He has been saving that amount each month just in case he needs extra money in the future to pay for something he hasn't thought of yet.

12 Total of fixed expenses. In this space, you write the total of all the fixed expenses for each month. Rich's total of his fixed expenses is $497.19 for January and $497.19 for February.

The second half of Rich's record of expenses is shown at the top of page 35. It lists Rich's **variable expenses**. Your variable expenses are more difficult to keep track of and plan for. They change from month to month. And they may also have to be paid at different times of the month.

By looking at Rich's record of variable expenses, you can see this information:

13 <u>Groceries</u>. In this space, Rich has listed the amount he spent for groceries each month. In January, for his food and other groceries, Rich spent $189.12. In February, he spent $182.41.

14 <u>Utilities</u>. Here, Rich has listed an expense of $58.11 for January and an expense of $31.41 for February. These amounts are what he paid for utilities, such as electricity, gas, and water, in those two months.

15 <u>Telephone</u>. The amount of Rich's phone bill for each month is listed in this space. In January, he paid $26.15. In February, he paid $30.43.

16 <u>Furniture</u>. In this space, Rich has listed what he spent for furniture—$45.16 in January and $64.09 in February.

17 <u>Clothes</u>. In this space, Rich has listed his expenses for clothes for both months. In January, Rich spent $84.14 on clothes. In February, he spent $39.94.

18 <u>Personal care</u>. Under "Personal care," you might list things that you buy to take care of yourself. This could include getting your hair cut and many things you might buy at the drug store. Rich has listed a personal care expense of $56.00 for the month of January. For February, he has listed an expense of $51.01.

19 <u>Transportation</u>. In this space, you would list all the expenses you have for your car during one month. Your gas bills would be part of this expense. So would anything you buy for your car, such as a new tire, or any work you have done on your car, such as a tune-up. If you don't have a car, the cost of riding the bus might be listed here. Or you might list any money you save each month to buy a new car. For car upkeep, Rich spent $124.00 in January and $63.44 in February.

	VARIABLE EXPENSES		
13	Groceries	189.12	182.41
14	Utilities	58.11	31.41
15	Telephone	26.15	30.43
16	Furniture	45.16	64.09
17	Clothes	84.14	39.94
18	Personal care	56.00	51.01
19	Transportation	124.00	63.44
20	Recreation and gifts	11.00	25.00
21	Other	24.18	51.86
22	**Total of Variable Expenses**	617.86	539.59
23	**TOTAL OF ALL EXPENSES**	1,115.05	1,036.78

20 Recreation and gifts. In this space, you would list the amount you spend for recreation and gifts. Recreation is what you do for fun, such as going to the movies or a ball game. For recreation and gifts, Rich spent $11.00 in January and $25.00 in February.

21 Other. "Other" is the space to list any other expenses you have each month that don't belong in any of the other spaces on the record of expenses. In this space, Rich has listed expenses of $24.18 for January and $51.86 for February.

22 Total of variable expenses. In this space, you write the total of all the variable expenses for each month. Rich's total of his variable expenses is $617.86 for January and $539.59 for February.

23 Total of all expenses. Here, you list the total of all expenses for each month. To do this, you add the total of the fixed expenses to the total of the variable expenses. For January, Rich's total of all expenses was $1,115.05. For February, it was $1,036.78.

By keeping good records, Rich was able to get a good idea of how much he spent each month. By looking at his record of expenses for January and February, you can see that he spends about $1,100.00 each month.

Budgeting Tip

It's hard to remember what all your expenses have been each month unless you keep a record as you go along. Find a way to do this and stick to it. One way is to buy a large file with pockets in it, like the one shown below. Label each pocket with the name of one kind of expense. Then make sure you get a receipt every time you spend money. When you can't get a receipt, make one yourself by writing the amount on a piece of paper. At the end of each day, put your receipts into the right pockets in your file. At the end of the month, your file will help you fill out your record of expenses.

FIGURE IT OUT

Look at the expenses listed below. Draw a circle around each one that is a variable expense and might change from one month to the next. Then use all the amounts listed here to finish filling out the record of expenses on page 37. Be careful. In some cases, you will have to add together two or more expenses to get the right amount for the record.

- Cotton shirt $15.96

- Rent for apartment $290.00

- Car insurance payment $34.85

- Food from Hi-Lo Market $64.36

- Birthday present $15.44

- Car loan payment $180.00

- Birthday present $21.08

- Rock concert tickets $24.00

- Bookcase rack $19.90

- Groceries from Cohen's Corner Store $57.51

- Haircut $12.00

- Emergency savings $30.00

- Gas credit card payment $41.90

- New pair of shoes $45.26

- Telephone bill $15.73

- Life insurance payment $22.18

- Donuts from the Nutty Donut $5.25

- Groceries from Hi-Lo Market $62.05

	March
FIXED EXPENSES Taxes: Federal	—
State	—
Property	—
Rent or mortgage payment	
Insurance: Health	28.00
Life	
Property	—
Car	
Loan Payments: Car	
Other	
Emergency savings fund	
Total of Fixed Expenses	
VARIABLE EXPENSES Groceries	
Utilities	50.79
Telephone	
Furniture	
Clothes	
Personal care	
Transportation	
Recreation and gifts	
Other	32.00
Total of Variable Expenses	
TOTAL OF ALL EXPENSES	

FIGURE IT OUT

Fill out your own record of expenses for one month. Save your receipts so that you have to do as little guessing as possible.

FIXED EXPENSES Taxes: Federal	
State	
Property	
Rent or mortgage payment	
Insurance: Health	
Life	
Property	
Car	
Loan Payments: Car	
Other	
Emergency savings fund	
Total of Fixed Expenses	
VARIABLE EXPENSES Groceries	
Utilities	
Telephone	
Furniture	
Clothes	
Personal care	
Transportation	
Recreation and gifts	
Other	
Total of Variable Expenses	
TOTAL OF ALL EXPENSES	

WORDS TO LEARN

average monthly expenses the amount of money spent in an average, or normal, month. Add together your monthly expenses for a number of months—for instance, six months. Then divide the total by the number of months. The amount you get will be your average monthly expenses.

When Rich first started making his budget, he found that his monthly expenses were different at different times of the year. In the winter, for example, Rich's utility bills were higher than they were during the summer months. This is because the weather is colder and Rich uses more gas to heat his apartment. Rich found that in the fall he pays more for clothing to get ready for the winter months. In the summer, Rich spends more money on recreation because there are more things to do. And in the spring, Rich often fixes things up in his apartment. That means he spends more in those months for furniture and other things he uses around the house. So Rich's expenses are never quite the same from one month to the next.

When you make a budget, it helps to know what your **average monthly expenses** are. This is the amount you spend in an average month. Like Rich, you will spend different amounts in different months. But if you figure out how much you spend in an average month, this will help you plan how much you need to meet your expenses. In Rich's case, he found his average monthly expenses by adding together all his monthly expenses for the entire year. Then he divided this amount by 12, the number of months in a year. Below, you can see the work Rich did to find his average monthly expenses.

Monthly Expenses	
Month	Expenses
January	$1,115.05
February	$1,036.78
March	$1,135.32
April	$1,083.92
May	$1,104.82
June	$1,099.19
July	$1,068.54
August	$1,229.23
September	$1,154.21
October	$1,180.54
November	$1,282.91
December	$1,298.31
Total	$13,788.82
Average Monthly Expense	$1,149.07

FIGURE IT OUT

Figure out your average monthly expenses by following these steps:

1. Fill out your record of expenses for three or more months. If you don't have receipts for everything in those months, make the best guesses you can about what you spend. Watch out for large bills that you pay in some months but not in others.

2. Find the total of all your expenses for each month. Then add these totals together.

3. Divide your answer by the number of months in your record. Write the amount you get in the space at the bottom of the page. It is your average monthly expenses.

Month						
FIXED EXPENSES Taxes: Federal						
State						
Property						
Rent or mortgage payment						
Insurance: Health						
Life						
Property						
Car						
Loan Payments: Car						
Other						
Emergency savings fund						
Total of Fixed Expenses						
VARIABLE EXPENSES Groceries						
Utilities						
Telephone						
Furniture						
Clothes						
Personal care						
Transportation						
Recreation and gifts						
Other						
Total of Variable Expenses						
TOTAL OF ALL EXPENSES						

Average monthly expenses: _____

5
What Is a Good Spending Plan?

It looks as if Les is still having trouble with his money. Rich did help him to figure out his income and his expenses. But Les does not understand how to make a good spending plan. Actually, there are no tricks to making a good spending plan, or budget—just plenty of planning. In this chapter, you will learn how to plan a budget. The work you did in chapters 3 and 4 will help you in this chapter. You will see why it is so important to plan a budget according to the way you live.

WORDS TO LEARN

balanced budget a budget in which the amount of money taken in is the same as or greater than the amount of money spent. If your income is the same as or more than your expenses, you have a balanced budget.

inflation a rise in costs (how much things cost to buy). When there is inflation, the same thing will cost more next year than it does now.

trial spending plan a test budget, or your first spending plan as you try to make a balanced budget.

As you can see, Les was having some trouble planning his budget. With Rich's help, however, he had figured out his monthly income and his average monthly expenses.

"The next step," Rich told Les, "is to make a **trial spending plan**."

Rich explained that a trial spending plan is really a test budget, or your first try to make a budget that works. Trial spending plans are made to be changed. What you want in the end is a **balanced budget**. This is a budget in which your monthly income, or the amount of money you take in each month, is greater than your expenses each month. You can probably expect to change your trial spending plan at least once before you have a balanced budget.

At first, a trial spending plan is just a record of your income and your average monthly expenses. It helps you compare what you earn to what you spend. On page 43 is the record that Rich made of his income and his average monthly expenses for one month. He figured out his average monthly expense for each expense on the record.

By looking at Rich's record of income and expenses, you can see the following information:

1 Rich's income for one month was $1,200.00. This includes all the money that Rich took home after his taxes were withheld.

2 As on his record of expenses in Chapter 4, Rich's expenses for the month are divided into fixed expenses and variable expenses.

3 Rich's fixed expenses include rent, insurance payments, and other payments that don't change from month to month.

4 The total for Rich's fixed expenses for the month is $497.19.

Record of Income and Expenses

1	INCOME	1,200.00
2	FIXED EXPENSES Taxes: Federal	—
	State	—
	Property	—
	Rent or mortgage payment	275.00
3	Insurance: Health	—
	Life	19.00
	Property	—
	Car	42.15
	Loan Payments: Car	91.04
	Other _school_	45.00
	Emergency savings fund	25.00
4	**Total of Fixed Expenses**	497.19
2	VARIABLE EXPENSES Groceries	202.35
	Utilities	50.40
	Telephone	34.75
	Furniture	40.40
5	Clothes	59.44
	Personal care	61.32
	Transportation	100.33
	Recreation and gifts	49.13
	Other	47.74
6	**Total of Variable Expenses**	645.86
7	**TOTAL OF ALL EXPENSES**	1,143.05

5 Rich's variable expenses include groceries, utilities, the telephone bill, clothes, personal care, transportation, recreation and gifts, and other costs that are different each month.

6 Rich's variable expenses for an average month come to a total of $645.86.

7 Rich found the total amount of his average monthly expenses by adding the total of his fixed expenses and the total of his variable expenses. Rich's record shows that he spends $1,143.05 in an average month.

Since Rich had a record of how much money he took in during the month and how much he spent, he could tell if his budget was balanced. To do this, he just subtracted his expenses from his income.

$$\begin{array}{r} \$1,200.00 \ \text{income} \\ - \ \$1,143,05 \ \text{expenses} \\ \hline \$ \quad 56.95 \ \text{money left} \end{array}$$

Rich found that he had $56.95 left that month. Since Rich's income was greater than his expenses, he had a balanced budget.

Rich liked having a balanced budget, and he wanted to keep having balanced budgets. So he decided to plan out his expenses and to try to make each monthly budget balance. Rich's plan, which was based on his record of income and average monthly expenses, became the trial spending plan you see on pages 45 and 46.

When Rich made his trial spending plan, he decided to use only dollars and not dollars and cents. He changed amounts like $42.15 and $91.04 to $43.00 and $92.00. This is called "rounding up." It's a good idea to do this when you make your spending plan. Whenever you have an amount that has dollars *and* cents, change it to the next highest dollar.

When he made his trial spending plan, Rich tried to figure out how his income and his expenses might change over the year. For example, he knew that he was supposed to get a raise in September. He figured out how much the raise might be, and he added that amount into his income for September through December. He also knew that his rent would go up in May and that his car loan payment would stop in November. He figured out what his new rent might be and added that amount into his rent expense for May through December. He did not list any amount for his loan payment in December.

Rich also knew that his variable expenses would go up. When expenses go up during a year, it is called **inflation**. There is really no way of knowing how much expenses will go up, but Rich could guess based on the inflation rate for the last few years. In his trial spending plan, Rich guessed that his expenses might go up 10 percent in one year's time. In other words, Rich figured that an expense such as the $203.00 he spends for groceries in an average month might become $224.00 in one year's time.

$203.00   average monthly expense for groceries
×   .10   inflation
$ 20.30   amount this expense might go up

$203.00   average monthly expense for groceries
+ $20.30   amount this expense might go up
$223.30   average monthly expense for groceries a year later

$224.00   rounded up

Of course, Rich was just guessing how much his expenses would go up. But he knew they probably would go up, and he wanted his spending plan to be as true to life as possible. So Rich listed his expenses *without* inflation for the first six months of his plan. For the last six months, he listed his expenses *with* inflation.

Trial Spending Plan

Month	January	February	March	April	May	June
INCOME	1,200.00	1,200.00	1,200.00	1,200.00	1,200.00	1,200.00
FIXED EXPENSES Taxes: Federal	—	—	—	—	—	—
State	—	—	—	—	—	—
Property	—	—	—	—	—	—
Rent or mortgage payment	275.00	275.00	275.00	275.00	295.00	295.00
Insurance: Health	—	—	—	—	—	—
Life	19.00	19.00	19.00	19.00	19.00	19.00
Property	—	—	—	—	—	—
Car	43.00	43.00	43.00	43.00	43.00	43.00
Loan Payments: Car	92.00	92.00	92.00	92.00	92.00	92.00
Other school	45.00	45.00	45.00	45.00	45.00	45.00
Emergency savings fund	25.00	25.00	25.00	25.00	25.00	25.00
Total of Fixed Expenses	499.00	499.00	499.00	499.00	519.00	519.00
VARIABLE EXPENSES Groceries	203.00	203.00	203.00	203.00	203.00	203.00
Utilities	51.00	51.00	51.00	51.00	51.00	51.00
Telephone	35.00	35.00	35.00	35.00	35.00	35.00
Furniture	41.00	41.00	41.00	41.00	41.00	41.00
Clothes	60.00	60.00	60.00	60.00	60.00	60.00
Personal care	62.00	62.00	62.00	62.00	62.00	62.00
Transportation	101.00	101.00	101.00	101.00	101.00	101.00
Recreation and gifts	50.00	50.00	50.00	50.00	50.00	50.00
Other	48.00	48.00	48.00	48.00	48.00	48.00
Total of Variable Expenses	651.00	651.00	651.00	651.00	651.00	651.00
TOTAL OF ALL EXPENSES	1,150.00	1,150.00	1,150.00	1,150.00	1,170.00	1,170.00
Amount overspent						
Amount left over	50.00	50.00	50.00	50.00	30.00	30.00

Trial Spending Plan

Month	July	August	September	October	November	December
INCOME	1,200.00	1,200.00	1,320.00	1,320.00	1,320.00	1,320.00
FIXED EXPENSES Taxes: Federal	—	—	—	—	—	—
State	—	—	—	—	—	—
Property	—	—	—	—	—	—
Rent or mortgage payment	295.00	295.00	295.00	295.00	295.00	295.00
Insurance: Health	—	—	—	—	—	—
Life	19.00	19.00	19.00	19.00	19.00	19.00
Property	—	—	—	—	—	—
Car	43.00	43.00	43.00	43.00	43.00	43.00
Loan Payments: Car	92.00	92.00	92.00	92.00	92.00	—
Other _school_	45.00	45.00	45.00	45.00	45.00	45.00
Emergency savings fund	25.00	25.00	25.00	25.00	25.00	25.00
Total of Fixed Expenses	519.00	519.00	519.00	519.00	519.00	427.00
VARIABLE EXPENSES Groceries	224.00	224.00	224.00	224.00	224.00	224.00
Utilities	57.00	57.00	57.00	57.00	57.00	57.00
Telephone	39.00	39.00	39.00	39.00	39.00	39.00
Furniture	46.00	46.00	46.00	46.00	46.00	46.00
Clothes	67.00	67.00	67.00	67.00	67.00	67.00
Personal care	69.00	69.00	69.00	69.00	69.00	69.00
Transportation	112.00	112.00	112.00	112.00	112.00	112.00
Recreation and gifts	56.00	56.00	56.00	56.00	56.00	56.00
Other	53.00	53.00	53.00	53.00	53.00	53.00
Total of Variable Expenses	723.00	723.00	723.00	723.00	723.00	723.00
TOTAL OF ALL EXPENSES	1,242.00	1,242.00	1,242.00	1,242.00	1,242.00	1,150.00
Amount overspent	42.00	42.00				
Amount left over			78.00	78.00	78.00	170.00

Rich's trial spending plan was a good one. You can tell this by looking at the amounts listed in the bottom two lines of his plan. Because his income and his expenses would change over the year, these amounts are not the same for every month. But Rich could see that in 10 of the months he should have money left over if he followed this plan. For two months, July and August, he would spend more money than he earned. But he could still pay for those extra expenses with some of the money left over from the first half of the year.

By knowing what you usually spend and what you have spent in the past, you can even out expenses like this. In Rich's case, for example, he could save some of the extra $50.00 and $30.00 in January, February, March, April, May, and June for when he needed an extra $42.00 in July and August. But the only way he could do this is by knowing what his average monthly expenses are and what his monthly expenses have been for each month in the past.

Budgeting Tip

No matter how well you add or subtract, making trial spending plans and budgets can leave you screaming. When you do so much math, it's easy to make a mistake. Save yourself lots of time and trouble. When you start planning a budget, make one of your first expenses a calculator.

FIGURE IT OUT

One of Rich's friends, Penny Pynchor, is also making a trial spending plan. Below is a month of Penny's plan. Finish adding up the expenses. Then see if she has a balanced budget.

Trial Spending Plan

INCOME	1,120.00
FIXED EXPENSES Taxes: Federal	200.00
State	40.00
Property	—
Rent or mortgage payment	235.00
Insurance: Health	15.00
Life	—
Property	—
Car	30.00
Loan Payments: Car	80.00
Other	—
Emergency savings fund	25.00
Total of Fixed Expenses	
VARIABLE EXPENSES Groceries	240.00
Utilities	35.00
Telephone	14.00
Furniture	36.00
Clothes	75.00
Personal care	40.00
Transportation	25.00
Recreation and gifts	15.00
Other	10.00
Total of Variable Expenses	
TOTAL OF ALL EXPENSES	
Amount overspent	
Amount left over	

Rich told Les that he was lucky his raise in salary would cover the amount that his expenses would go up over the year. "If my salary didn't go up enough to cover my expenses," Rich said, "I would have to find some way to cut my expenses."

Rich would not be able to cut down on most of his fixed expenses. Usually, his fixed expenses are ones that he *has* to pay in certain amounts. For example, Rich's largest fixed expense is his rent, and this is an expense that is not easy to change. The only way Rich could lower his rent would be to move to another apartment, and even this may not always work. He might not be able to find an apartment with a lower rent. And even if he did find an apartment where he could pay less rent each month, he might end up spending more to move than he would save on rent.

One item on the fixed expense list that might seem unusual to you is the emergency savings fund. This fund is for money that is saved up to be used in case of an emergency. An emergency would be some large expense that you didn't plan for. The emergency savings fund is listed under the fixed expenses because the best way to save up the money you need for such a fund is to save a fixed amount of money each month. That way, you know there will be some money in the savings account in case you need it. Having an emergency savings fund makes sense because, no matter how well you plan your spending, you can never be sure of all the things that might happen. This is *not* an expense that you should cut from your budget if your budget doesn't balance.

If Rich did have to cut back on the money he was spending, the best place to cut would be in his variable expenses. For example, if he shut off his lights when he was not using them, fixed his leaky hot water faucet, and wore sweaters instead of turning up the heat, he would be sure to save some money on his utilities. In the same way, he could learn how to shop in stores that were having sales. Then he would save money on food, clothes, and personal care products. In other words, Rich could fix his spending plan so that it fitted the way he lived and so that the money he made matched the expenses he had to pay.

FIGURE IT OUT

Below is the trial spending plan Les made for one month. Finish adding up the expenses. Then compare the total of all expenses with Les's income. If Les's total expenses are the same as or less than his income, then he has a balanced budget.

Trial Spending Plan

INCOME	1,200.00
FIXED EXPENSES Taxes: Federal	—
State	—
Property	—
Rent or mortgage payment	290.00
Insurance: Health	—
Life	29.00
Property	—
Car	56.00
Loan Payments: Car	96.00
Other	—
Emergency savings fund	35.00
Total of Fixed Expenses	
VARIABLE EXPENSES Groceries	280.00
Utilities	65.00
Telephone	50.00
Furniture	60.00
Clothes	125.00
Personal care	75.00
Transportation	125.00
Recreation and gifts	50.00
Other	30.00
Total of Variable Expenses	
TOTAL OF ALL EXPENSES	
Amount overspent	
Amount left over	

FIGURE IT OUT

It looks as if Les will have to cut back on some of his expenses in order to make his budget balance. Look back at what you wrote on page 50. The amount Les overspent is the amount he needs to cut from his budget.

Les should begin by lowering some of his variable expenses. Whenever you cut your variable expenses, it's a good idea to trim a little from each one. In this case, it would probably be good for Les to see if he could make his spending plan work by cutting between 5 and 10 percent from his variable expenses. You figure out 5 percent of an amount by multiplying that number by .05. You figure out 10 percent of an amount by multiplying that number by .10. Below, Les has begun to figure out what his variable expenses would be if he cut 10 percent from each one. Finish his work for him by doing the following:

1. Figure out what the new amount would be for each of Les's variable expenses, rounding up to the nearest dollar.
2. Find the new total of Les's variable expenses.
3. Add this to the total of Les's fixed expenses to get the new total for all his expenses.
4. Compare the new total for all his expenses to Les's income. Subtract the smaller number from the larger one. The answer will show whether or not Les's budget now balances.

VARIABLE EXPENSES	
Groceries	280.00
Utilities	65.00
Telephone	50.00
Furniture	60.00
Clothes	125.00
Personal care	75.00
Transportation	125.00
Recreation and gifts	50.00
Other	30.00
Total of Variable Expenses	860.00

Amount – 10 percent = New amount

280.00 – 28.00 =
65.00 – ~~6.50~~ 7.00 =
50.00 – 5.00 =
60.00 – 6.00 =
125.00 – ~~12.50~~ 13.00 =
75.00 – ~~7.50~~ 8.00 =
125.00 – ~~12.50~~ 13.00 =
50.00 – 5.00 =
30.00 – 3.00 =

New total of variable expenses _____
Total of fixed expenses + _____

Total of all expenses _____

_____ Total of all expenses
– _____ Income

_____ Amount overspent
(The budget still doesn't balance.)

OR

_____ Income
– _____ Total of all expenses

_____ Amount left over
(The budget now balances.)

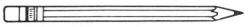

FIGURE IT OUT

Trial Spending Plan

	After Cutting 10 percent	
INCOME	1,200.00	
FIXED EXPENSES Taxes: Federal	—	
State	—	
Property	—	
Rent or mortgage payment	290.00	
Insurance: Health	—	
Life	29.00	
Property	—	
Car	56.00	
Loan Payments: Car	96.00	
Other	—	
Emergency savings fund	35.00	
Total of Fixed Expenses	506.00	
VARIABLE EXPENSES Groceries	252.00	
Utilities	58.00	
Telephone	45.00	
Furniture	54.00	
Clothes	112.00	
Personal care	67.00	
Transportation	112.00	
Recreation and gifts	45.00	
Other	27.00	
Total of Variable Expenses	772.00	
TOTAL OF ALL EXPENSES	1,278.00	
Amount overspent	78.00	
Amount left over		

Here is what Les's spending plan looked like after he cut 10 percent from each variable expense. Les still needs to cut $78.00 from his spending plan before he has a balanced budget. You'll learn more in the next chapter about ways to cut each kind of expense. For now, make your own plan to lower Les's expenses by the final $78.00. You could take away another 5 or 10 percent from his variable expenses. Or you might take a large amount from one or two of the expenses. At the bottom of the page, give reasons for the way you chose.

_____

_____

_____

_____

_____

Trial Spending Plan

	Original Amount	New Amount
INCOME	1,200.00	1,200.00
FIXED EXPENSES Taxes: Federal	—	—
State	—	—
Property	—	—
Rent or mortgage payment	290.00	290.00
Insurance: Health	—	—
Life	29.00	29.00
Property	—	—
Car	56.00	56.00
Loan Payments: Car	96.00	96.00
Other	—	—
Emergency savings fund	35.00	25.00
Total of Fixed Expenses	506.00	496.00
VARIABLE EXPENSES Groceries	280.00	240.00
Utilities	65.00	55.00
Telephone	50.00	40.00
Furniture	60.00	50.00
Clothes	125.00	100.00
Personal care	75.00	65.00
Transportation	125.00	110.00
Recreation and gifts	50.00	40.00
Other	30.00	—
Total of Variable Expenses	860.00	700.00
TOTAL OF ALL EXPENSES	1,366.00	1,196.00
Amount overspent	166.00	
Amount left over		4.00

Les and Rich went over Les's trial spending plan together. Rich helped Les find ways to cut his variable expenses and still be able to buy many of the things Les needs and wants to have. For example, Les cut $15.00 from his transportation expenses, but he will still be able to save a little each week toward his goal of buying a motorcycle. Also, Les cut $10.00 from his emergency savings fund, but he will still save $25.00 each month in case of emergencies. At the left is the spending plan Rich and Les made.

Since this is a *trial* spending plan, Les will use these figures to try to save money on his expenses. Les may find that he can't live on $240.00 a month for groceries. If this happens, then Les will have to lower some of his other expenses and add the amount he saves there to how much he can spend on groceries.

As Les looked over his trial spending plan, however, he had one other question. He asked Rich how he would know if he was staying within his trial spending plan.

Rich used Les's groceries as an example, and he explained how a trial spending plan can help Les control the money he spends on groceries. Rich told Les that if he planned to spend $240.00 a month on groceries, that meant he should be spending one-fourth of that amount each week.

$240.00 ÷ 4 = $60.00

In other words, he would spend $60.00 a week on groceries. One good way for Les to keep to his spending plan is to allow himself $60.00 to spend on groceries that week—and *only* that amount. He might even keep the $60.00 in a separate envelope. Then, each time he went shopping for groceries, he could spend money only from that envelope.

If Les finds he can get by with less than $60.00 for groceries, then he can put this extra money in a savings account or use it for other expenses where he may be short of money. If he finds that he needs more money, he will have a good idea of how much more he needs if he has been watching his expenses each week.

In order to stick to a budget, it is also important to go on keeping records of what you spend each month. If you have been saving your receipts in a file folder each month, you should go on doing that. And at the end of each month, you should fill out a budget form like the one below. It's like the form for a trial spending plan, but the budget form lets you compare the amount of money you planned for each expense to the amount of money you really spent. It shows you if your spending plan is working or not. And it helps you to see quickly which expenses you are having problems with.

Budget

Month	January		February		March		April		May		June	
	Budgeted	Spent	Budgeted	Spent	Budgeted	Spent	Budgeted	Spent	Budgeted	Spent	Budgeted	Spent
FIXED EXPENSES Taxes: Federal												
State												
Property												
Rent or mortgage payment												
Insurance: Health												
Life												
Property												
Car												
Loan Payments: Car												
Other												
Emergency savings fund												
Total of Fixed Expenses												
VARIABLE EXPENSES Groceries												
Utilities												
Telephone												
Furniture												
Clothes												
Personal care												
Transportation												
Recreation and gifts												
Other												
Total of Variable Expenses												
TOTAL OF ALL EXPENSES												
Amount over budget												
Amount under budget												

FIGURE IT OUT

Look back at the amounts you wrote down for your income and your expenses in chapters 3 and 4. Then make your own trial spending plan. Subtract the total of your expenses from your income to see if you have a balanced budget.

If you don't have a balanced budget, then follow these steps one at a time:

1. Cut all your variable expenses by 5 percent. (To see how to do this, look at page 51.)

2. If you are still spending too much, cut your variable expenses by 10 percent instead of 5 percent.

3. If your budget still won't balance, think about each variable expense. Are some less important to you than others? Cut these expenses even more.

Trial Spending Plan

INCOME				
FIXED EXPENSES Taxes: Federal				
State				
Property				
Rent or mortgage payment				
Insurance: Health				
Life				
Property				
Car				
Loan Payments: Car				
Other				
Emergency savings fund				
Total of Fixed Expenses				
VARIABLE EXPENSES Groceries				
Utilities				
Telephone				
Furniture				
Clothes				
Personal care				
Transportation				
Recreation and gifts				
Other				
Total of Variable Expenses				
TOTAL OF ALL EXPENSES				
Amount overspent				
Amount left over				

FIGURE IT OUT

Look back at the balanced budget in your trial spending plan on page 55. Write that budget again here in each of the columns marked "Budgeted." Then use this budget form for your records. At the end of each month, write how much you really spend for each expense. It will help show you if you have a good spending plan.

Budget

Month	Budgeted	Spent	Budgeted	Spent	Budgeted	Spent	Budgeted	Spent	Budgeted	Spent	Budgeted	Spent
FIXED EXPENSES Taxes: Federal												
State												
Property												
Rent or mortgage payment												
Insurance: Health												
Life												
Property												
Car												
Loan Payments: Car												
Other												
Emergency savings fund												
Total of Fixed Expenses												
VARIABLE EXPENSES Groceries												
Utilities												
Telephone												
Furniture												
Clothes												
Personal care												
Transportation												
Recreation and gifts												
Other												
Total of Variable Expenses												
TOTAL OF ALL EXPENSES												
Amount over budget												
Amount under budget												

6

Can You Make Your Budget Better?

Planning a budget is just the first step. Getting the budget to work is another. Les has been trying to make his spending plan fit into his way of life. With a little help from his friend Rich, he probably will. But it may take practice.

Most budgets take some time before they start to work really well. A budget needs to be tested. The only way to test a budget is to use it. When you use your budget, you can see how it works and how it doesn't work. Then you can figure out how to make your budget better.

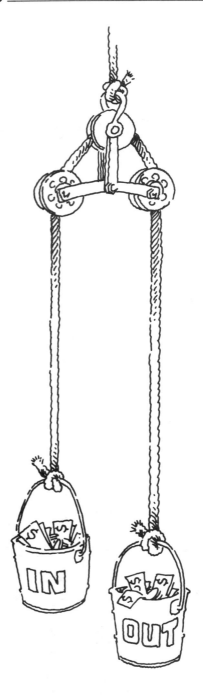

In Chapter 5, you learned that one of the goals of budgeting is to keep a balanced budget. The money that you take in must be the same as or more than the amount you spend. You don't want your expenses to be greater than your income.

When you made your spending plan, you probably thought it would be easy to follow it. After all, according to your plan, there should be no problem paying for all your expenses with what you earn. But what happens when you start following your plan? If you are like most people, you may have a little trouble getting your plan to work.

When Les made his spending plan, he planned to spend $60.00 a week on food. But Les soon found he was spending more than $60.00 for food each week. In fact, he was spending closer to $65.00. And that meant he didn't have enough money for some of the other things in his spending plan. Once he couldn't pay a bill on time. And his money problems seemed to be growing. Les's budget no longer balanced. His spending plan wasn't working.

"When your spending plan doesn't work," Rich told Les, "the first thing to do is to find out *why*."

Les was spending more on food than he had planned. On the top of page 59 are some questions that Rich asked Les.

- "Do you look for low prices on food?"
- "Do you need all the food you buy?"
- "Are you wasting the food that you do buy?"
- "Can you buy different kinds of food that don't cost so much?"
- "Can you find food stores with lower prices than where you are shopping?"

You can tell a lot from the answers to these questions. If Les answered no to one of the first two questions, he might be spending more than he needs to on food. If he answered yes to one of the last three questions, he is also probably spending too much. Changing one or two of these food-buying habits would help. It might bring his weekly food bill down to $60.00.

But Les was a smart shopper when it came to food. He shopped at large food stores that had low prices. He didn't buy special cuts of meat or other things that cost a lot. And when he bought food, he bought only what he needed. And he used all the food he bought. Food prices had gone up since Les had made his spending plan. That was what the problem was. Even with careful shopping, it was clear that his food was going to cost him $65.00 a week.

"So now what do I do?" Les wanted to know.

"The next thing to do," Rich explained, "is to look over your spending plan. Study each part of it. Compare your spending plan to your receipts that tell you what you are really spending. Look for places where you are spending less money each month than you had planned. In other words, can you use money from one part of your spending plan to pay for another expense?"

Les studied his budget carefully and checked his receipts, too. He found that he did need $20.00 more each month for groceries. He also found that he was not spending all he had planned to spend for personal care products. Below, you can see how much Les had planned to spend on personal care products and how much he really spent.

VARIABLE EXPENSES		
Groceries	240.00	
Utilities	55.00	
Telephone	40.00	
Furniture	50.00	
Clothes	100.00	
Personal care	65.00	43.00
Transportation	110.00	
Recreation and gifts	40.00	
Other	—	

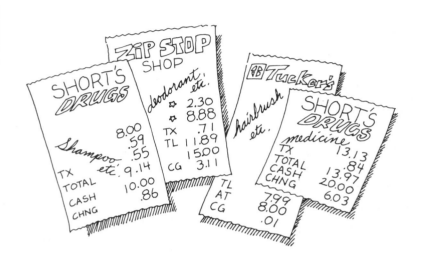

By looking over what he had planned to spend and what he was really spending, Les was able to see that he could move some money from one part of his budget to another. He could spend $22.00 less each month on personal care products. He had been spending about $43.00 on personal care products each month since he started his budget, and he had planned to spend $65.00. The $22.00 he saved on personal care products each month would help pay the extra money he needed for his groceries.

Changing your spending plan like this is a common way to make a budget work. As you have already seen, it is difficult to know ahead of time just how well your spending plan will work. You really have to try it out—give it a chance—and then see where you might need to make some changes. This is exactly what Les was doing, and it's what you will do as you make your budget better.

FIGURE IT OUT

Rita doesn't feel as though she has control of her money. She makes her budget balance each month, but she always has to take some money out of what she planned to put into her emergency savings fund. She's worried that if an emergency does come up, she won't have enough money to pay for it.

Look over the amount Rita has budgeted and spent for each expense. Put a check mark next to three expenses for which Rita is spending too much money for both months.

Budget

Month	September		October	
	Budgeted	Spent	Budgeted	Spent
FIXED EXPENSES Taxes: Federal	247.00	247.00	247.00	247.00
State	62.00	62.00	62.00	62.00
Property				
Rent or mortgage payment	300.00	300.00	300.00	300.00
Insurance: Health	40.00	40.00	40.00	40.00
Life				
Property				
Car	40.00	40.00	40.00	40.00
Loan Payments: Car	120.00	120.00	120.00	120.00
Other				
Emergency savings fund	40.00	22.00	40.00	23.00
Total of Fixed Expenses	849.00	831.00	849.00	832.00
VARIABLE EXPENSES Groceries	260.00	280.00	260.00	310.00
Utilities	40.00	42.00	40.00	35.00
Telephone	25.00	23.00	25.00	19.00
Furniture	35.00	41.00	35.00	0
Clothes	105.00	128.00	105.00	122.00
Personal care	67.00	75.00	67.00	80.00
Transportation	44.00	40.00	44.00	39.00
Recreation and gifts	75.00	40.00	75.00	63.00
Other				
Total of Variable Expenses	651.00	669.00	651.00	668.00
TOTAL OF ALL EXPENSES	1,500.00	1,500.00	1,500.00	1,500.00
Amount over budget		0		0
Amount under budget		0		0

FIGURE IT OUT

Do *you* have control of your money? Can you make your budget better? Look back at the record you made of your budget on page 56. Compare what you have been spending to the amounts that you budgeted for each month. See if you have any problem spots, or expenses where you will have to find ways to start spending less money. Put a check mark next to each expense listed below where you are almost always spending more than you planned. At the bottom of the page, write down ideas you have about ways to cut your spending for those expenses.

Fixed Expenses
　Taxes
　　Federal
　　State
　　Property
　Rent or mortgage payment
　Insurance
　　Health
　　Life
　　Property
　　Car
　Loan payments
　　Car
　　Other
　Emergency savings fund

Variable Expenses
　Groceries
　Utilities
　Telephone
　Furniture
　Clothes
　Personal care
　Transportation
　Recreation and gifts
　Other

Ideas for cutting spending: _____

_____

_____

_____

_____

_____

Moving money from one place in your budget to another as Les does will solve some budget problems. But it won't always work. Sometimes you may be spending all the money you planned—and more. The answer then may be to cut back what you are spending.

If you want to cut back what you are spending, the best place to start is with your variable expenses. For most people, food is the largest variable expense they have. Not all of them are smart shoppers like Les and Rich. Below are some shopping tips. They show you how to get the most for your money at the grocery store.

Grocery Shopping Tips

- Make a shopping list and buy only those things on the list. Never buy more than you need.
- Avoid impulse shopping, or shopping without planning first. Never buy food when you are hungry.
- Look for specials, or things with prices that are lower than usual. Buy mostly things with prices that are marked down.
- Save coupons that offer money off when you buy certain products. Then try not to buy those products without using the coupons.
- Buy the larger sizes of things such as laundry soap. Often, the larger size gives you more for your money.
- Buy generic products, or ones that don't have a company name on the box or can. Generic products cost less.

If you are a smart shopper, you probably do most of the things in this list. You may already do them all. But if you don't, take a few minutes to look them over. They are also good rules to follow to cut other expenses. Careful shopping will save you money on personal care products, clothing, furniture, and other things that you buy all the time.

VARIABLE EXPENSES	
Groceries	
1 Utilities	
2 Telephone	
3 Furniture	
4 Clothes	
5 Personal care	
6 Transportation	
7 Recreation and gifts	
8 Other	
Total of Variable Expenses	
TOTAL OF ALL EXPENSES	
Amount over budget	
Amount under budget	

You can lower your other variable expenses, too, with a little work. Here are some ideas for how you might cut some money from each of your other variable expenses.

1 Utilities. Contact your local utilities company to find out what ideas they have for saving energy. Don't use energy if you don't need it. If you have a gas heater, turn off the pilot light during the hot months of the year.

2 Telephone. Make your long-distance calls at times of the day when it costs less. Try not to make long telephone calls. You might make a rule about how many minutes your telephone calls can be.

3 Furniture. Check out garage sales and used-furniture stores for good deals on furniture. But be sure the furniture you buy is sturdy and will last. Remember, used furniture is a good deal only if it can be used for a while longer by you.

4 Clothes. Don't buy clothes you don't need, and take good care of the clothes that you have so that they will last. When you do buy clothes, look for stores that are having big sales so that you can save money. And sometimes you can find a good deal on used clothes at a secondhand shop or bargain shop.

5 Personal care. Buy generic personal care products, or products that don't have a company name on them. Try to buy things on sale or in large sizes.

6 Transportation. Use buses or carpools to get to and from work or school. When your car needs service, don't always take it to the dealer. Many times, smaller garages will do the same work on your car for a lower price. Be careful to take good care of your car, so that you don't get surprised by large repair costs. And learn how to do simple car care, such as changing the oil and rotating the tires.

7 Recreation and gifts. Go to parks for recreation or to other places that won't cost you as much money as the movies. Make your own gifts to give as presents.

8 Other. Just stick more closely to your budget and don't let yourself do any of the "other" things that are costing you money. This is a space for extras. If you're trying to cut costs, the extras should be one of the first expenses to cut.

Another way to make a spending plan work is to cut your fixed expenses. Cutting fixed expenses, however, is not that easy. After all, these expenses are called "fixed" because they do not change. Taxes, insurance, and loan payments, for example, may be impossible to change. It is possible, though, to lower your fixed expenses with a little thinking and some hard work. Below are ideas you can try that might help you cut your fixed expenses.

9 Federal and state income taxes. Save all receipts for any expenses that have to do with your job. These receipts might help you at tax time. Find a tax expert or tax service to help you plan the best way to save on your income taxes.

10 Rent or mortgage payment. For rent or lease payments, you might offer to work off part of the payment. For example, you might offer to clean up around your apartment building each week in exchange for a slightly lower rent. For house payments, talk over the details carefully with the loan officer when you set up such payments. Find out if there are any ways to cut costs in those payments.

11 Health insurance. Look into different kinds of health insurance plans to see which plan would be best for you and would not cost too much. Keep yourself fit by exercising and keeping your weight down, so that you don't cause health problems for yourself.

12 Life insurance. Look into which life insurance plan fits your needs best. Many plans may offer you more than you need and cost more than you should be paying.

13 Property insurance. Renters can get renter's insurance. This will protect the things in your home, and it doesn't cost very much. Homeowners should be careful when they pick out property insurance. Talk to a few companies, so that you get the best buy.

14 Car insurance. There are many kinds of car insurance. Talk to agents at several companies to find out which company has the lowest rates. Think over what might or might not happen to your car. Decide if you want to get collision *and* comprehensive insurance. Many times, car insurance ends up costing you more than it might save you when you have an accident.

15 Loan payments. Don't be afraid to shop around for the best deal on a loan. Many times, you can get lower payments at your own bank or at a credit union. Don't borrow money for things you don't need. Try to wait until you can afford them without a loan.

	FIXED EXPENSES	
9	Taxes: Federal	
	State	
	Property	
10	Rent or mortgage payment	
11	Insurance: Health	
12	Life	
13	Property	
14	Car	
15	Loan Payments: Car	
	Other	
	Emergency savings fund	
	Total of Fixed Expenses	

FIGURE IT OUT

Look back at the things you checked on page 62. Those were places where you thought you might be spending too much. Decide which costs you need to cut and then write your new budget here. Use the lines at the right to make notes about any steps you need to take to help make your new budget work. For example, you might cut your expenses for books, listed under "Other," by going to the library more.

I will change my spending by:

_____

_____

_____

_____

_____

_____

_____

_____

_____

_____

_____

_____

_____

_____

_____

_____

_____

_____

_____

Budget

INCOME	
FIXED EXPENSES Taxes: Federal	
State	
Property	
Rent or mortgage payment	
Insurance: Health	
Life	
Property	
Car	
Loan Payments: Car	
Other	
Emergency savings fund	
Total of Fixed Expenses	
VARIABLE EXPENSES Groceries	
Utilities	
Telephone	
Furniture	
Clothes	
Personal care	
Transportation	
Recreation and gifts	
Other	
Total of Variable Expenses	
TOTAL OF ALL EXPENSES	

7 How Well Is Your Budget Working?

Les may seem not to understand, but in this book he has learned how to plan a budget, how to keep a budget, and how to change a budget to make it work.

Les also learned how important it was to stick to his budget. After all, no matter how carefully Les might have planned a budget, he had to stick to his plans. If he didn't follow his plans, then all his work would not help him reach his financial goals.

Reaching financial goals is the main reason for making a budget and sticking to it. As Rich pointed out, once a person decides what these goals are, making a budget and keeping to that budget is the best way to reach these financial goals.

Here are some of the financial goals Les wrote when he started planning his budget.

One-Year Goals

Buying new tires for the car

Taking music lessons

Going skiing every other weekend during the winter

Two-Year Goals

Going to college to take night classes

Buying a new motorcycle

Buying a color television

Five-Year Goals

Taking a trip to Europe

In order for Les to reach his goals, he learned that he had to make a spending plan, try out his plan, and fix his plan to fit the way he really spent his money. Then he had to make a budget that he could stick to in his everyday living.

Les also learned that he had to practice control over how he spends his money. This does not mean that Les had to starve himself or go without shoes in the winter. But it does mean that Les had to learn to spend his money carefully as he tried to keep his budget balanced.

Trial Spending Plan

	Original Amount	New Amount	
INCOME	1,200.00	1,200.00	
FIXED EXPENSES Taxes: Federal	—	—	
State	—	—	
Property	—	—	
Rent or mortgage payment	290.00	290.00	
Insurance: Health	—	—	
Life	29.00	29.00	
Property	—	—	
Car	56.00	56.00	
Loan Payments: Car	96.00	96.00	
Other	—	—	
Emergency savings fund	35.00	25.00	**1**
Total of Fixed Expenses	506.00	496.00	
VARIABLE EXPENSES Groceries	280.00	240.00	
Utilities	65.00	55.00	
Telephone	50.00	40.00	
Furniture	60.00	50.00	
Clothes	125.00	100.00	
Personal care	75.00	65.00	
Transportation	125.00	110.00	**2**
Recreation and gifts	50.00	40.00	**3**
Other	30.00	—	
Total of Variable Expenses	860.00	700.00	
TOTAL OF ALL EXPENSES	1,366.00	1,196.00	
Amount overspent	166.00		
Amount left over		4.00	

Les's spending plan went through many changes before he had a balanced budget that he could follow.

1 Les cut the amount he put into his emergency savings fund. Still, he was able to save $25.00 each month. This was an important part of Les's budget. After nearly a year, he had more than $200.00 in his emergency savings fund. This was money he would need if any emergencies came up.

2 Only part of the $110.00 budgeted for transportation each month paid for gas for Les's car. Les also saved some of this $110.00 each month. The money he saved paid for the new tires he needed and would one day give him enough money to buy a new motorcycle like Rich's.

3 Les also saved some of his gifts money each month. He did this because he knew that he would need the extra money to pay for music lessons when he started them. He also wanted to save enough money to buy a guitar.

4 Les changed his plan to fit the way he lived. When he found he was spending too much on groceries, he looked at what he was spending on other things each month. He found that he always spent much less than he planned on personal care products. He used that money to help pay for the extra cost of groceries.

VARIABLE EXPENSES Groceries	240.00		
Utilities	55.00		
Telephone	40.00		
Furniture	50.00		
Clothes	100.00		
Personal care	65.00	43.00	**4**
Transportation	110.00		
Recreation and gifts	40.00		
Other	—		

FIGURE IT OUT

You've seen how Les has managed to make a balanced budget. How well is your budget working? Look back over your records and answer the following questions to find out.

1. List your one-year, two-year, and five-year financial goals here. (You may want to look back at the list you wrote on page 15.)

   One-year goals: _____

   _____

   _____

   Two-year goals: _____

   _____

   _____

   Five-year goals: _____

   _____

   _____

2. Which one-year goals do you think you will be able to reach soon?

   _____

   _____

3. How long do you think it will take you to reach your other financial goals?

   Goal   *Years/Months*

   _____

   _____

   _____

   _____

   _____

4. Which part of your budget is not working? Why?

   _____

   _____

   _____

   _____

5. What plans do you have to make this part of your budget work?

_____

_____

_____

_____

6. Which part of your budget is working better than you thought it would? Why?

_____

_____

_____

_____

7. What do you plan to do with any extra money you might have?

_____

_____

_____

_____

8. List some ways you might still be able to cut your expenses.

_____

_____

_____

_____

9. List one reason why keeping a budget is not easy for you.

_____

_____

10. What changes, if any, do you still need to make in your life to make your budget work better?

_____

_____

_____

_____

Of course, making and keeping a budget are not simple things to do. Here are a few last hints to help make your work easier.

- Keep good records of your income and expenses.
- Keep a file folder to organize your receipts.
- Make a spending plan that fits the way you live.
- Be willing to fix your spending plan to fit the expenses you have.
- Know that changing your spending plan is not a sign of failure. It is a step toward finding a budget that works for you.
- Do your work on your budget on a regular schedule. Try to work on your budget at the same time and in the same place each week.
- Use a calculator when you are working on your budget.
- Stick to your budget. If you are not able to, find out what part of your budget is not working and why.
- Let yourself splurge once in a while. When you splurge, you let yourself buy something without thinking too much about it. Of course, if you do this too much or do this with really expensive things, this can ruin your budget. But if you splurge only once in a while, it will help you to stick to your budget at other times.
- And remember, it always pays to plan.

FIGURE IT OUT

Here is one more budget form to help you plan your income and your expenses. Look back at parts of this book if you have any trouble. Remember to keep careful records, so that you control your money and move toward your financial goals.

Budget

Month	Budgeted	Spent	Budgeted	Spent	Budgeted	Spent	Budgeted	Spent	Budgeted	Spent	Budgeted	Spent
FIXED EXPENSES Taxes: Federal												
State												
Property												
Rent or mortgage payment												
Insurance: Health												
Life												
Property												
Car												
Loan Payments: Car												
Other												
Emergency savings fund												
Total of Fixed Expenses												
VARIABLE EXPENSES Groceries												
Utilities												
Telephone												
Furniture												
Clothes												
Personal care												
Transportation												
Recreation and gifts												
Other												
Total of Variable Expenses												
TOTAL OF ALL EXPENSES												
Amount over budget												
Amount under budget												

Answers

Page 5
Answers will come from your own ideas.

Page 10
Answers will come from your own ideas.

Page 13
Answers will come from your own ideas.

Page 15
Answers will come from your own ideas.

Page 21
1. a. $52.00   b. $260.00   c. $1,040.00
   d. $13,520.00

2.

Worker	Hourly Wage	Hours Worked in a Pay Period	Steady Income for Each Pay Period
Sara	$6.58	160	$1,052.80
William	$5.02	140	$702.80
Alice	$5.50	70	$385.00
Maria	$4.32	40	$172.80
Eric	$7.10	80	$568.00

3. $2,060.00
4. $18,000.00

Page 25
1.

September					
Pay Period	Base Salary	Amount Sold	Commission	Money Earned as Commission	Weekly Salary
9/2–9/8	$240.00	$390.50	2 percent	$7.81	$247.81
9/9–9/15	$240.00	$293.91	2 percent	$5.88	$245.88
9/16–9/22	$240.00	$589.02	2 percent	$11.78	$251.78
9/23–9/29	$240.00	$785.00	2 percent	$15.70	$255.10

Monthly Salary: $1,001.17

2. 9/9–9/15, $245.88
3. 9/23–9/29, $255.70
4. $1,001.17

Page 27
1. a. $3,000.00   b. four

2. a. $400.00   b. $1,600.00   c. $550.00
   d. $2,200.00   e. 13

3. a. $4.00   b. $6.00   c. $64.00

Page 28

List A

"I make anywhere from $250.00 to $500.00 each week. It all depends on how much I sell. I do know I will get at least $200.00 a week, guaranteed."

"I make $800.00 a month, every month, by working a 40-hour week, every week."

"I get $50.00 for every chair I make. I can usually make two chairs a day. My boss pays me a salary according to how many chairs I make."

"I charge a certain amount of money for each job I complete."

List B

This person has a steady income.

This person earns a variable income and charges a fee for the work he or she does.

This person earns a variable income but also has a base salary.

This person has a variable income and is paid piecework wages.

Page 29 or 30
Answers will come from your own facts and figures.

Page 36
- Cotton shirt $15.96
- Rent for apartment $290.00
- Car insurance payment $34.85
- Food from Hi-Lo Market $64.36
- Birthday present $15.44
- Car loan payment $180.00
- Birthday present $21.08
- Rock concert tickets $24.00
- Bookcase rack $19.90
- Groceries from Cohen's Corner Store $57.51
- Haircut $12.00
- Emergency savings $30.00
- Gas credit card payment $41.90
- New pair of shoes $45.26
- Telephone bill $15.73
- Life insurance payment $22.18
- Donuts from the Nutty Donut $5.25
- Groceries from Hi-Lo Market $62.05

Page 37

	March
FIXED EXPENSES Taxes: Federal	—
State	—
Property	—
Rent or mortgage payment	290.00
Insurance: Health	28.00
Life	22.18
Property	—
Car	34.85
Loan Payments: Car	180.00
Other	
Emergency savings fund	30.00
Total of Fixed Expenses	585.03
VARIABLE EXPENSES Groceries	189.17
Utilities	50.79
Telephone	15.73
Furniture	19.90
Clothes	61.22
Personal care	12.00
Transportation	41.90
Recreation and gifts	60.52
Other	32.00
Total of Variable Expenses	483.23
TOTAL OF ALL EXPENSES	1,068.26

Page 38

Answers will come from your own facts and figures.

Page 40

Answers will come from your own facts and figures.

Page 48

Trial Spending Plan

INCOME	1,120.00
FIXED EXPENSES Taxes: Federal	200.00
State	40.00
Property	—
Rent or mortgage payment	235.00
Insurance: Health	15.00
Life	—
Property	—
Car	30.00
Loan Payments: Car	80.00
Other	—
Emergency savings fund	25.00
Total of Fixed Expenses	625.00
VARIABLE EXPENSES Groceries	240.00
Utilities	35.00
Telephone	14.00
Furniture	36.00
Clothes	75.00
Personal care	40.00
Transportation	25.00
Recreation and gifts	15.00
Other	10.00
Total of Variable Expenses	490.00
TOTAL OF ALL EXPENSES	1,115.00
Amount overspent	
Amount left over	5.00

Page 50

Trial Spending Plan

INCOME	1,200.00
FIXED EXPENSES Taxes: Federal	—
State	—
Property	—
Rent or mortgage payment	290.00
Insurance: Health	—
Life	29.00
Property	—
Car	56.00
Loan Payments: Car	96.00
Other	—
Emergency savings fund	35.00
Total of Fixed Expenses	506.00
VARIABLE EXPENSES Groceries	280.00
Utilities	65.00
Telephone	50.00
Furniture	60.00
Clothes	125.00
Personal care	75.00
Transportation	125.00
Recreation and gifts	50.00
Other	30.00
Total of Variable Expenses	860.00
TOTAL OF ALL EXPENSES	1,366.00
Amount overspent	166.00
Amount left over	

Page 51

		Amount	− 10 percent	= New amount
VARIABLE EXPENSES Groceries	280.00	280.00	− 28.00	= 252.00
Utilities	65.00	65.00	− 6.50 7.00	= 58.00
Telephone	50.00	50.00	− 5.00	= 45.00
Furniture	60.00	60.00	− 6.00	= 54.00
Clothes	125.00	125.00	− 12.50 13.00	= 112.00
Personal care	75.00	75.00	− 7.50 8.00	= 67.00
Transportation	125.00	125.00	− 12.50 13.00	= 112.00
Recreation and gifts	50.00	50.00	− 5.00	= 45.00
Other	30.00	30.00	− 3.00	= 27.00
Total of Variable Expenses	860.00			

New total of variable expenses   772.00
Total of fixed expenses +   506.00

Total of all expenses   1,278.00

1,278.00	Total of all expenses	1,200.00	Income
−1,200.00	Income	− _____	Total of all expenses
78.00	Amount overspent (The budget still doesn't balance.)	_____	Amount left over (The budget now balances.)

OR

Page 52

Answers will come from your own ideas. You might try taking 10 percent more out of Les's variable expenses, but he still wouldn't have a balanced budget. Some variable expenses, such as groceries, clothes, and recreation and gifts, might be lowered even more. The expense for "Other" might be cut to zero. Also, Les may have to cut back a little on the amount of money he plans to put into his emergency savings fund each month.

Page 55

Answers will come from your own facts and figures.

Page 56

Answers will come from your own facts and figures.

Page 61

Budget

Month	September		October	
	Budgeted	Spent	Budgeted	Spent
FIXED EXPENSES				
Taxes: Federal	247.00	247.00	247.00	247.00
State	62.00	62.00	62.00	62.00
Property				
Rent or mortgage payment	300.00	300.00	300.00	300.00
Insurance: Health	40.00	40.00	40.00	40.00
Life				
Property				
Car	40.00	40.00	40.00	40.00
Loan Payments: Car	120.00	120.00	120.00	120.00
Other				
Emergency savings fund	40.00	22.00	40.00	23.00
Total of Fixed Expenses	849.00	831.00	849.00	832.00
VARIABLE EXPENSES				
✓ Groceries	260.00	280.00	260.00	310.00
Utilities	40.00	42.00	40.00	36.00
Telephone	25.00	23.00	25.00	19.00
Furniture	35.00	41.00	35.00	0
✓ Clothes	105.00	128.00	105.00	122.00
✓ Personal care	67.00	75.00	67.00	80.00
Transportation	44.00	40.00	44.00	39.00
Recreation and gifts	75.00	40.00	75.00	63.00
Other				
Total of Variable Expenses	651.00	669.00	651.00	668.00
TOTAL OF ALL EXPENSES	1,500.00	1,500.00	1,500.00	1,500.00
Amount over budget		0		0
Amount under budget		0		0

Page 62

Answers will come from your own facts and figures and your own ideas.

Page 66

Answers will come from your own facts and figures and your own ideas.

Pages 70 and 71

Answers will come from what has happened to you with your budget.

Page 73

What you write here will come from your own facts and figures. The important thing is to have a balanced budget that works for you.